TREES
OF SOUTHERN AFRICA
A FIRST FIELD GUIDE

Page 16

Page 30

ELSA POOLEY

Contents

Umbrella Thorn, *Acacia tortilis*

First edition published in 1999 by
Struik Publishers (Pty) Ltd
(a member of Struik New Holland
Publishing (Pty) Ltd)
80 McKenzie Street,
Cape Town 8001

2 4 6 8 10 9 7 5 3 1

Registration No.: 54/00965/07

ISBN 1 86872 291 0

Editor: Gary Lyon
Designer: Dominic Robson

Reproduction: Disc Express Cape (Pty) Ltd
Printed: CTP Book Printers (Pty) Ltd

Photographic credits: Gerald Cubitt: front
cover (left, top right); B. Olbrich: p. 36;
Jo Onderstall: front cover (right), pp. 3, 11,
12, 17, 19, 24 (right), 27, 33, 41, 43; Kristo
Pienaar: back cover (left, right), p. 1
(right), 18, 21, 32, 37, 39, 48; D. M.
Richardson: front cover (bottom right), pp. 7
(left), 10, 16, 44; Piet van Wyk: pp. 1 (left),
2, 5, 6, 7 (right: top to bottom), 8, 9, 13, 14,
15, 20, 22, 23, 24 (left), 25, 26, 28, 29, 30,
31, 34, 35, 38, 40, 42, 45, 46, 47, 49, 50, 51,
52, 53, 54, 55.

Introduction

Trees play a vital role in the environment and are a distinctive feature of many landscapes. They hold soil and prevent heavy water runoff thereby reducing soil erosion. Trees also provide food and shelter for animals, insects and man and shade and support for other plants; they absorb carbon dioxide and they produce the oxygen we breathe. They also beautify our gardens and cities and provide people with fuel, building materials, furniture, household implements, medicines and manufactured goods, such as paper and rubber.

Learning about trees can be exciting and very interesting. It can be pursued almost anywhere, with the added bonus that trees do not run or fly away!

This book introduces the reader to a selection of the larger, more common or attractive trees found in southern Africa. It is hoped that the descriptions of the 55 species in this book will encourage further study and enable the reader to identify trees with ease in the field.

Common Tree Euphorbia, *Euphorbia ingens*

What is a tree?

The South African National Tree List broadly defines a tree as a woody plant that grows at least 2 m tall, and includes larger woody shrubs and climbers.

In southern Africa we have a remarkably diverse tree flora comprising 1 700 indigenous[G] tree species. In addition, there are about 100 alien tree species in the region. Some of these have become naturalised[G], but many of them are invasive[G].

Trees have many shapes, sizes and growth habits. Some are deciduous[G], losing all their leaves in seasons when water is in short supply. Others are evergreen[G], retaining their leaves in all seasons but losing individual leaves as they become old.

Identifying trees

In order to identify trees one needs to observe the following features very carefully:

Height and **shape** of the tree, and colour of the crown (leaves).

Colour and **texture** of the bark.

Shape and **size** of the **leaves** and their arrangement on the stem. Check to see if leaves are **simple** or **compound** and note whether the margin is toothed or not.

   Is the leaf a typical leaf? Young leaves at the base of the tree are often larger, with a different shape to those found on more mature or established branches. If the tree is deciduous[G], check on the ground beneath it for fallen leaves, which can be used for identification of the tree.

Hairiness of the leaves or branches.

Latex or **milky sap** present or not if a stem, branch or leaf vein is cut or damaged.

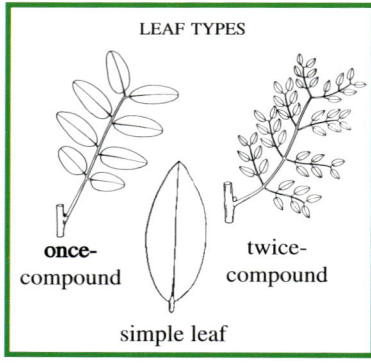

LEAF TYPES

once-compound

twice-compound

simple leaf

Check the **locality** and **habitat**, for example, savanna, forest or grassland etc., and use the distribution maps. Also note the tree's abundance in the area.

   It is important to remember that trees change with the seasons. Many trees are deciduous[G] and their leaves change colour in autumn (Apr–May) before falling off in winter (May–August). Most trees flower in spring (Sept–Oct).

   Some species can be identified by their **flowers** or **growth form** alone. Shape, size and colour of flowers and fruits are also important features to consider.

Distinctive trees

The following trees are distinctive and can be easily identified by just one or two characteristic features.

Pod Mahogany (207), *Afzelia quanzensis*, a medium to tall deciduous[G] tree with a spreading, flattish crown, found in dry woodland and sand forest. Flowers have a single large reddish petal[G] and pods are brown and woody.

Peeling Plane/Lekkerbreek (483), *Ochna pulchra*, a small to medium tree with a twisted trunk and a roundish crown. The characteristic smooth grey bark peels, leaving cream to whitish-green patches. The fruits are flower-like with enlarged reddish sepals[G]. They have three fleshy, kidney-shaped seeds which ripen from cream to shiny black.

Natal Wild Banana (34), *Strelitzia nicolai*, a decorative banana- or palm-like tree growing in clumps. Found from coastal dunes to inland evergreen forests.

Lala Palm (23), *Hyphaene coriacea*, erect or reclining palm tree with leathery fan-like leaves or fronds. Found in low altitude woodland, forming extensive stands especially in coastal grassland in Maputaland.

Wild Gardenia (691), *Gardenia volkensii*, a small, usually multi-stemmed deciduous[G] tree, with a dense, much branched crown. It is covered in beautiful fragrant white flowers in spring which later turn yellow. Found in woodland.

Pompon Tree (521), *Dais cotinifolia*, a lovely small, slender flowering tree with a rounded crown. Flowers are clustered in pink, pompon-like flowerheads[G]. It is quite widespread in forest margins, thicket, and rocky valleys.

Halfmens (649), *Pachypodium namaquanum*, found in desert and semi-desert. A spiny, cactus-like tree with a crown of large leaves usually at the top of a single, tall trunk. Resembles a person standing upright (see p. 8).

Sausage Tree (678), *Kigelia africana*, a handsome medium to large tree with a straight trunk and spreading rounded crown. Flowers are large and wine-coloured or maroon. Fruits are large, fleshy and sausage-like in appearance. It is found on floodplains and in riverine vegetation.

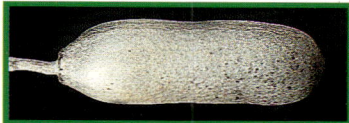

Cork Bush (226), *Mundulea sericea*, a decorative shrub or small tree with pale corky bark. Leaves are grey-green with silvery hairs. Flowers are sweetpea-like and pink to purple in colour. It is found in woodland, and on sandy soils.

How to use this book

Each species account is divided into several headings. These are explained below:

Common name The English name by which the tree is known. Numbers in brackets after the common name refer to the tree's number as provided on the 'South African Tree List'. If preceded by the letter 'Z' the number given refers to that of 'Zimbabwe's Tree List'.

Scientific name Derived from Greek or Latin, it is the internationally recognised name, written in italics. It is made up of a genus (plural: genera), reflecting a group of similar species, for example, *Erythrina,* and a specific name which identifies a separate species, for example, *lysistemon.* This two-part name is part of a larger *family* unit, for example, Fabaceae, which groups genera with characters in common.

African names The names in Afrikaans (A), North Sotho (NS),

Halfmens,
Pachypodium namaquanum

Swazi (Sw), Venda (V), Xhosa (X) and Zulu (Z) have been supplied where possible.

Height The overall height, in metres, as well as the leaf, flower and fruit size, in millimetres. For leaf, flower and fruit (pod), measurements are given as length and width (for example, 125 x 5 mm) unless otherwise stated. Note that size varies enormously within species in trees, and these measurements should be taken as a guide, not the rule.

Identification Characteristic features of the tree which distinguish it from others. Also given are flowering and fruiting times in brackets, for example (Apr–Jul), where applicable. Remember that flowers and fruits are not available throughout the year, but will help to confirm identification when present. It is, however, possible to identify a tree from its leaves.

Habitat The habitat or vegetation type where the tree is commonly found. Distribution maps are shaded in green and orange to indicate species that are endemic^G and indigenous^G respectively.

Ecological notes Notes on how the plant is utilised by people, animals, birds and insects, and its role in the natural environment.

Status Whether the tree is protected by law. One that is may not be damaged or removed without a permit.

Gardening A brief guide to propagation and suitability of trees for the garden.

Similar species Closely related species and very similar species are mentioned where relevant.

The letter ^{G} after a word means that it appears in the glossary on page 56.

Where a scientific name is followed by another scientific name in brackets, for example, *Acacia erioloba* (=*Acacia giraffae*), the name in brackets is the previous name by which the tree was known.

Umbrella Thorn, *Acacia tortilis*

Acacia erioloba (=A. giraffae)

African names:
Kameeldoring (A);
mogôtlhô (NS).

Height: A small to large (2–16 m) tree, usually with a sturdy trunk, and a widely spreading, fine but dense crown.

Identification: The bark is rough and deeply grooved. Leaves are twice compound, with grey-green leaflets, up to 13 mm long. The paired thorns, up to 60 mm long, are straight, sturdy and swollen at the base. Flowers occur in small, scented, yellow balls (Jul–Sep). Pods are large, thick, hard and velvety grey, about 120 x 70 mm, and do not split open (Dec–Apr).

Habitat: Found in arid woodland, favouring sandy soils.

Ecological notes: A valuable shade tree, it is conspicuous in the arid semi-desert northwest. The pods are eaten by livestock and game and the gum is edible. Bark and pods are used in traditional medicine. The timber is hard, and is useful for firewood and for mine props.

Status: Protected.

Gardening: Slow growing, from seed. Drought and frost resistant.

Similar species: Candlepod Acacia (170) *Acacia hebeclada* (up to 7 m). A small spreading shrub or tree with creamy white flowers. Two subspecies, *hebeclada* and *chobiensis,* have thick, woody pods held erect. A third subspecies, *tristis*, has hanging pods.

Sweet Thorn 172

Acacia karroo

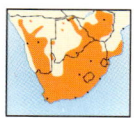

African names: Soetdoring (A); mookana (NS); umunga (X, Z).

Height: Usually a medium-sized (4–10 m, can reach 20 m), deciduous^G tree, with a spreading, rounded crown.

Identification: The bark is rough with narrow grooves; young branches are rusty red. The paired thorns are straight and white, 30–250 mm long. Leaves are twice compound with feathery, dark green leaflets, up to 10 x 5 mm. Flowers occur in masses of scented, yellow balls near the branch tips (Oct–Feb). Pods are sickle-shaped, up to 160 x 10 mm (Jan–May).

Habitat: One of the most widespread trees in southern Africa, often found in large stands.

Ecological notes: The pods and leaves are good fodder for livestock and game, and the gum is edible. The flowers attract masses of insects, which in turn attract birds. The timber is used for furniture, fence posts and firewood; the bark for tanning, making rope and, with the roots, in traditional medicine.

Status: Protected in Northern Cape and Free State.

Gardening: Fast growing, from seed. Frost and drought resistant.

Similar species: Scented Thorn (179) *Acacia nilotica* (3–6 m). Has a flattish crown; the bark is blackish-grey and deeply grooved; the pods are like a string of beads and are scented.

Umbrella Thorn

Acacia tortilis

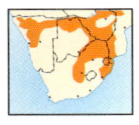

African names:
Haak-en-steek (A);
mosu (NS);
isithwethwe (Sw, Z);
umsasane (Z).

Height: A small to medium or large (5–20 m), deciduous[G] tree, usually single-stemmed; has a flat, spreading crown.

Identification: Older trees have a characteristic flat crown (see p. 9). The bark is rough, grey-black. Thorns are either in hooked or straight pairs, or in mixed pairs. Leaves are twice compound and are amongst the smallest in the acacias, with very fine leaflets, up to 2 mm long. Flowers are in small, white balls (Oct–Feb). Pods are spirally twisted, creamy-brown and hang in clusters (Mar–Jul).

Habitat: Savanna woodland and grassland.

Ecological notes: The bark, leaves and pods provide good fodder for livestock and game. The gum is eaten by animals and people, and the green seeds by parrots, monkeys and baboons. The wood is a useful all-purpose timber and makes good firewood. The bark is used to make rope and in traditional medicine.

Status: Protected in Northern Cape and Free State.

Gardening: Grown from seed. Drought and frost resistant.

Fever Tree

Acacia xanthophloea

African names: Koorsboom (A); mooka-kwena (NS); umhlafunga (Sw, Z); umhlosinga, umkhanyagude (Z).

Height: A medium to tall (10–30 m), deciduous[G] tree with a tall trunk and a sparse, spreading crown.

Identification: Often grows in groves. Bark is smooth, greenish-yellow and powdery. The paired spines are straight and white. Leaves are small and twice compound. Flowers are fragrant and are in yellow balls (Sep–Nov). Pods are straight, flat and papery (Jan–Apr).

Habitat: Hot, dry, low-lying areas near rivers, lakes and swamps.

Ecological notes: The flowers, leaves and branches are browsed by game. The bark is used in traditional medicine. The wood can be used as an all-purpose timber.

Gardening: Quick growing, from seed. Sensitive to frost and cold.

Baobab 467

Adansonia digitata

African names: Kremetart (A); motsoo (NS).

Height: A deciduous[G] tree (10–25 m) with a massive trunk (up to 12 m in diameter) and a sparse, spreading crown.

Identification: The bark is thick, smooth and folded, shiny greyish-pink; the branches taper upwards. Leaves are digitately compound (shaped like the fingers of a hand) and have 3–9 (average 5) large, shiny leaflets. The lovely large, waxy white flowers, up to 200 mm in diameter, hang below the branches (Oct–Dec). Fruits are large and oval, up to 150 mm long, and have a hard woody shell covered in velvety, yellowish hairs; the flesh is soft and tasty (Apr–May).

Habitat: Dry woodland.

Ecological notes: The leaves, flowers and fruits are browsed by livestock and game. The roots are tapped for water, the young roots and leaves are eaten by people, and the seeds are used as a coffee substitute. Elephants strip the stem for moisture. Fibre from the bark is used for rope, nets, baskets and clothing. The bark is used in traditional medicine.

Status: Protected.

Gardening: Grown from seed, popular for bonsai. Sensitive to cold and frost.

Flatcrown 148

Albizia adianthifolia

African names:
Platkroon (A);
muomba-ngoma (V);
umgadawenkawu,
umhlandlothi (X, Z);
usolo, igowane,
umbhebhele (Z).

Height: A tall (10–25 m),
deciduous[G] tree with a straight
trunk and a large, spreading,
flattish crown.

Identification: The bark is
yellowish grey-brown; the young
growth is covered with dense
brownish hairs. Leaves are large
and twice compound, up to
250 mm long, the dark green
leaflets are rectangular,
up to 20 x 8 mm. Flowers
form fluffy, powder-puff
blooms which are cream
tinged with pinkish-green
(Aug–Dec). Pods are flat
and pale brown, up to
150 x 35 mm (Sep–Feb).

Habitat: Coastal bush,
woodland, forest margins.

Ecological notes: The leaves are
browsed by elephants. The pods
and seeds are eaten by antelope.
The flowers attract butterflies.
The wood is used as an all-purpose
timber. The bark and root are used
in traditional medicine.

Gardening: Grows quickly from
seed, in frost free areas.

Similar species: Large-leaved
False Thorn (158) *Albizia
versicolor* (up to 20 m) has a
spreading, rounded crown; the
leaflets are large, up to 65 x 45
mm; the pods are shiny red-brown.

Aloe dichotoma

African names: Kokerboom (A).

Height: A succulent tree (3–7 m) with a sturdy trunk and a dense, roundish crown.

Identification: The trunk is up to 1 m in diameter at the base, tapering upwards; bark is smooth and yellowish, splitting and peeling with age. Branches are spreading and the leaves are held erect. Flower spikes^G are yellow, up to 300 mm long, and are held above the leaves (Jun–Jul).

Habitat: Rocky ridges in desert or semi-desert.

Ecological notes: Birds, mammals and insects are attracted to the copious nectar. The soft branches were once used by the San to make quivers for arrows, hence the common name.

Status: Protected.

Gardening: Grown from seed, it requires dry conditions.

Similar species: Giant Quiver Tree (30) *Aloe pillansii*, has fewer, more erect branches, the leaves curving downwards and flowers hanging below the leaves. Tree Aloe (28) *Aloe barberiae* (=*A. bainesii*) (10–18 m) has a rounded crown; it is found in wooded valleys and thicket in the eastern parts of the region; the flowers are pinkish-red.

Tree Wisteria

Bolusanthus speciosus

African names:
Vanwykshout (A);
mogapa (NS);
umhohlo (Sw, Z);
muswinga-phala (V).

Height: A graceful, small to medium-sized (4–12 m) tree. Deciduous^G with a fairly straight or multi-stemmed trunk, a narrow crown and drooping leaves.

Identification: The bark is dark, rough and deeply grooved. Leaves are compound and drooping; the shiny leaflets are unequal sided, tapering to a slender pointed tip. Violet-blue flowers, hanging in clusters up to 300 mm long, usually appear before the leaves do (Aug–Jan). Pods, up to 100 x 10 mm, are thin, flat and papery (Sep–Mar).

Habitat: Woodland (moist savanna), often on heavy soils.

Ecological notes: The leaves are browsed by game and the flowers are eaten by monkeys. The bark is used in traditional medicine. The timber is hard and termite resistant. It is good for fence poles and small pieces of furniture.

Status: Protected.

Gardening: Easily grown from seed, and popular for bonsai. Frost resistant.

Shepherd's Tree

Boscia albitrunca

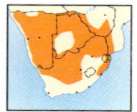

African names: Witgat (A); mohlôpi (NS); muvhombwe (V); umvithi (Z).

Height: A small (3–7 m) tree with a sturdy, twisted, single trunk and a neat, rounded crown.

Identification: The bark is smooth and whitish-grey. Leaves are clustered on stiff side-twigs and are tough and leathery, up to 50 x 15 mm, with a sharp tip. The small, greenish-yellow, scented flowers have no petals[G] and are produced in profusion (Aug–Nov). Fruits, up to 10 mm in diameter, are yellowish and berry-like (Nov–Apr).

Habitat: Widespread in dry woodland, often on termite mounds and in semi-desert.

Ecological notes: It is heavily browsed by livestock and game. The flowers attract insects. Birds and animals eat the fruits. Butterfly caterpillars (larvae) feed on the leaves. The roots are used as a coffee substitute and for porridge. The leaves and roots are used in traditional medicine.

Status: Protected.

Gardening: Grown from seed and root cuttings. Frost resistant.

Similar species: Stink Shepherd's Tree (124) *Boscia foetida*, has smaller leaves, 10–25 mm; the flowers and wood are unpleasantly scented. Karroo Shepherd's Tree (128) *Boscia oleoides*; leaves are not clustered; the flowers have 2–4 petals[G].

Msasa z252

Brachystegia spiciformis

African names: Msasa.

Height: A medium to large (8–18 m), deciduous^G tree with a tall trunk and a spreading crown.

Identification: The tree is conspicuous in spring when it is covered in a beautiful flush of pinkish-red leaves. Leaves are large and compound (4 pairs of leaflets with unequal bases), drooping and dark shiny green, the terminal pair of leaflets being the largest, up to 80 x 45 mm. Flowers are small and clustered in spikes^G, up to 60 mm long (Aug–Nov). Woody pods, up to 140 mm long, are hidden amongst the leaves (May–Aug).

Habitat: Dominant in miombo woodland (moist savanna).

Ecological notes: The flowers produce copious nectar, the source of a good honey. Butterfly caterpillars (larvae) feed on the leaves. The wood is used for firewood and the bark fibre for rope. Used in traditional medicine.

Gardening: Slow growing if grown from seed.

Similar species: Mfuti (Z248) *Brachystegia boehmii*, has feathery foliage and 13–28 pairs of narrow, oblong leaflets. Munondo (Z260) *Julbernardia globiflora*, has a rounded crown, leaves are compound and have 6 pairs of leaflets, the terminal ones are not the largest; the pods are velvety and are held above the leaves.

White Stinkwood 39

Celtis africana

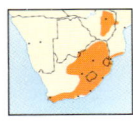

African names:
Camdeboo Stinkwood (E); Witstinkhout (A); molutu (NS); umvumvu (X, Z); ndwandwazane (Z).

Height: A medium to large (up to 30 m), deciduous[G] tree. In forest it is tall with a straight, sometimes buttressed, trunk. In the open it is short, with a spreading crown.

Identification: The bark is smooth and pale grey. Leaves are alternate and are bright green when young, becoming dark green when mature with 3 main veins from the unequal (asymmetric) base; the margins are usually toothed on the upper two thirds. Flowers are small, with male and female flowers on separate trees (Aug–Oct). Small, yellow berries, 6 mm in diameter, hanging on long, slender stalks, are produced in profusion (Oct–Feb).

Habitat: Widespread in forest, woodland and grassland.

Ecological notes: Browsed by livestock and game. The fruits are eaten by birds, baboons and monkeys. The flowers and fruits attract insects. The wood is used as an all-purpose timber. Used in traditional medicine.

Status: Protected.

Gardening: A popular garden, street and bonsai tree, grown from seed. Drought and frost resistant.

Similar species: Pigeonwood (42) *Trema orientalis* (5–15 m) is a common tree; the leaves are toothed along the whole margin. The fruits have very short stalks.

Cape Chestnut

Calodendrum capense

African names:
Wildekastaiing (A);
mookêlêla (NS);
umbhaba (X, Z).

Height: A medium to large
(8–25 m), evergreen^G or
deciduous^G tree with a tall straight
trunk and a rounded crown. It is
spectacular when in full flower.

Identification: The trunk is
up to 1 m in diameter; the
bark is smoothish and grey.
Leaves are large and simple,
and are arranged opposite
each other; they are hairless,
with scattered gland dots
(clear dots when held against
the sun), and are citrus
scented when crushed.
Lovely pink flowers with
dark maroon speckles are
held in large sprays up to
200 mm long (Jul–Mar,
mostly Oct–Jan). Fruit is a
large, rough, woody capsule
which splits open into 5
lobes^G containing large
black seeds (Jan–May).

Habitat: Forest and riverine thicket.

Ecological notes: The flowers and
leaves attract insects. The seeds
are eaten by monkeys and birds.
The timber is used for furniture,
turning, shelving and implements.

Gardening: An excellent street
or garden tree, it is grown from
seed or cuttings. It flowers when
quite young.

Mopane

Colophospermum mopane

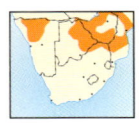

African names:
Mopanie (A);
mopane (NS).

Height: A medium to tall (up to
18 m, can reach 30 m), deciduous[G]
tree or multi-stemmed shrub.

Identification: The bark is grey-
brown and deeply grooved. Leaves
are compound and resemble
butterfly wings, and smell of
turpentine when crushed. Autumn
leaves are reddish-brown. Flowers
are greenish-white, in slender
spikes[G] (Oct–Mar). Pods, up to
70 x 20 mm, are pale brown and
flattened, and do not split open
(Mar–Jun). The seed is covered
in sticky, red, gland dots.

Habitat: Woodland, on sandy
soils, forming almost pure stands.

Ecological notes: Browsed by
livestock and game, especially
elephants. Caterpillars (larvae)
feed on the leaves, especially those
of the mopane worm (Emperor
moth), which then provide food for
people, birds and animals. The
durable timber is used for
furniture, building and firewood.

Gardening: Grown from seed;
frost sensitive.

Similar species: Large False
Mopane (199) *Guibourtia
coleosperma* (16–20 m) is mostly
restricted to Kalahari sands; the
leaflets are sickle-shaped; pods
dark brown, splitting open on the
tree and the red-covered seed hangs
out of the pod. Small False
Mopane (200) *Guibourtia
conjugata* (7–9 m). A deciduous[G]
tree with smooth bark; the leaflets
have rounded tips; the pods are
flat, almost round, and do not split
open; the seeds have no gland dots.

Red Bushwillow 532

Combretum apiculatum

African names: Rooibos (A); mohwelere (NS); umbondwe (Z).

Height: A small to medium-sized (3–6 m, can reach 10 m) tree. Deciduous[G] with a short, crooked trunk; often multistemmed from the base, with a sparse, spreading crown.

Identification: The bark is greyish-black, cracked and flaking with age. Leaves are opposite and hairless and turn brownish-red to golden-yellow in autumn, up to 140 x 80 mm, the tips ending abruptly in a slender, twisted point. The young growth is sticky. Flowers are creamy and scented and crowded in spikes, up to 70 mm long (Sep–Feb). The 4-winged fruits, 30 x 25 mm, are sticky when young, and yellowish-green to reddish-brown (Jan–May).

Habitat: Widespread, often dominant in woodland on well-drained soils in the northern parts of southern Africa.

Ecological notes: The leaves are browsed by game and cattle, and are used in traditional medicine. Flowers attract insects which attract birds. Parrots eat the seeds. Butterfly caterpillars feed on the leaves. The timber is hard, fine-grained and termite resistant; it is used for fence posts and firewood.

Gardening: Grown from seed; cold but not frost resistant.

Similar species: Velvet Bushwillow (537) *Combretum molle* (4–12 m) has dark, rough bark; the leaves are thick and rough with conspicuous net veins below. Young leaves are velvety. The fruits are 15–20 mm in diameter.

Commiphora harveyi

African names: Rooistamkanniedood (A); ihlunguthi (X); umbumbungane, uminyela (Z).

Height: A small to medium-sized (5–15 m), deciduous^G tree with a tall, broad, often twisted trunk and a sparse, spreading crown.

Identification: The greenish bark is conspicuous with large, peeling, papery, coppery-bronze pieces. No spines are present. Leaves are large and compound with 2–3 pairs of lateral leaflets and a terminal one. Leaves are shiny, dark green turning yellow in autumn. Fruits are round, up to 10 mm in diameter, and pale green ripening to red (Nov–Mar).

The seed is covered with a 4-lobed red aril^G (Nov–Mar).

Habitat: Coastal and dry forest, often in rocky places.

Ecological notes: The fruits are eaten by monkeys and birds, the heartwood is eaten by people and animals in times of drought. The wood is soft, and is used for traditional household implements.

Gardening: Grown from truncheons, it makes a good bonsai.

Similar species: Forest Corkwood (291) *Commiphora woodii* (5–20 m) has a straight, broad trunk and greenish-white bark (not peeling). The seed has a cup-shaped aril^G.

Common Cabbage Tree 564

Cussonia spicata

African names: Gewone kiepersol (A); umsenge (Sw, Z); mosêtshê (NS).

Height: A small to medium-sized (4–18 m), evergreen^G tree with a sturdy trunk and much branched, rounded crown.

Identification: The bark is corky. Leaves are large, up to 700 mm in diameter, dark green and clustered towards the ends of the branches; they are twice compound, the leaflets sometimes cut to the midrib^G. The small green flowers are clustered on thick spikes^G in branched terminal flowerheads^G (a double umbel^G), which are held above the leaves (Apr–May). Fruits are tightly packed and are small, 6 mm, purplish-green and fleshy (Jun–Sep).

Habitat: Widespread in woodland (moist savanna), grassland, on rock outcrops and on forest margins.

Ecological notes: The leaves are browsed by livestock and game, the roots and bark by black rhino, bushpigs and baboons. Flowers and fruits attract butterflies and birds. The roots are used in traditional medicine.

Status: Protected.

Gardening: Grown from seed or truncheons, it needs protection from cold winds.

Similar species: Transvaal Cabbage Tree (564.3) *Cussonia transvaalensis*, has a sparsely branched crown and blue- to grey-green leaves.

Jackal-berry

Diospyros mespiliformis

African names: Jakkalsbessie (A); motlouma (NS); umtoma (Sw); musuma (V).

Height: A medium to large (10–25 m), evergreen^G tree with a tall, bare, fluted trunk and a dense, spreading crown.

Identification: The bark is dark brown and grooved. Leaves are shiny dark green, simple and oblong in shape with wavy margins. They turn golden-yellow in autumn. Flowers are small, white and bell-shaped; male and female on separate trees (Oct–Nov). Fruits are fleshy, round and yellow, up to 25 mm in diameter, with a bristle-tip; the sepals^G of the flower are retained on the fruit (Apr–Sep). The fruit pulp is jelly-like and tasty.

Habitat: Bushveld, near rivers and streams, often on termitaria.

Ecological notes: The leaves are browsed by game. Fruits are eaten by game, birds and people and are used to brew beer. Butterflies breed on this tree. Wood is used for all-purpose timber, dugout canoes and stamping blocks. Leaves and bark are used in traditional medicine.

Status: Protected.

Gardening: Fast growing from seed, in frost-free areas.

Wild Pear 471

Dombeya rotundifolia

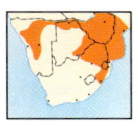

African names: Drolpeer (A); mohlabaphala (NS); umwane (Sw); tshiluvhari (V); inhlizinyonkhulu (Z).

Height: An attractive, small (3–10 m), deciduous[G] tree with showy flowers, a slender trunk and a sparse, spreading crown.

Identification: The bark is rough, deeply grooved and dark grey-brown. Leaves are large, thick and rough, dark green in colour and roundish, 30–150 mm in diameter, with 5–7 veins from the base. Masses of white to pale pink flowers, up to 20 mm in diameter, cover the tree – appearing before the leaves in spring (Jul–Sep). The fruit is a hairy nutlet[G] contained within the dry, brown petals[G] of the flower (Oct–Dec).

Habitat: Widespread in woodland, often found growing on rocky mountain slopes.

Ecological notes: The leaves are sometimes browsed by game. The flowers attract bees and butterflies. The inner bark is used for twine, and along with the bark, the root is used in traditional medicine. The wood is heavy and tough, and makes a useful all-purpose timber.

Gardening: A lovely garden, street and bonsai tree; fast growing, from seed and cuttings. Drought and frost tolerant.

Similar species: Natal Wild Pear (469) *Dombeya cymosa* (2–5 m) has pale grey bark. The leaves are small and thin, the flowers less than 13 mm in diameter (Mar–May).

Cape Ash 298

Ekebergia capensis

African names: Essenhout (A); mmidibidibi (NS); umgwenyezinja (X); umnyamathi (Sw, Z); umthoma, uvungu (Z).

Height: A medium to large (10–35 m), evergreen^G or semi-deciduous tree with a tall, sometimes fluted trunk (in forest) and a spreading, rounded crown.

Identification: The bark is grey-brown, smooth to rough and flaking. Young branchlets have raised, whitish dots and are marked with scars from fallen leaves. Leaves are compound and hanging, with 3–5 pairs of leaflets and a terminal one. Flowers are small, and in sprays, up to 80 mm long; male and female flowers occur on separate trees (Sep–Dec). Fruits are red, round and fleshy, 15–20 mm in diameter (Nov–Apr).

Habitat: In forests.

Ecological notes: The leaves are browsed by livestock and game. Butterflies and moths are attracted to the tree. Fruits are popular with birds, baboons and monkeys. The timber is suitable for furniture if treated. Bark, root and leaves are used in traditional medicine.

Status: Protected.

Gardening: Fast growing, from seed. Frost sensitive.

Similar species: Wild Plum (361) *Harpephyllum caffrum* (12–35 m) has leaves in whorls, crowded at the ends of thick branchlets. The leaves are firm, not hanging, with sickle-shaped leaflets. The large red fruits are oblong (25 mm long).

Transvaal Milkplum

Englerophytum magalismontanum

African names:
Stamvrug (A);
mohlatswa (NS);
umnumbela (Sw, V);
umthongwane (Z).

Height: Small to medium-sized tree (2–4 m, can reach 10 m). Evergreen[G] with a short, crooked trunk and a dense, dark green, rounded crown.

Identification: The smoothish, grey bark has small bumps on which the flowers and fruits appear. Branchlets are covered in silvery-brown hairs. Leaves are large, up to 140 x 50 mm, shiny, dark green above, densely covered in reddish-brown hairs beneath, and crowded towards the ends of the branchlets. The pinkish-brown flowers are strongly scented (Jun–Oct). The red fruits, up to 25 x 28 mm, are densely crowded on the trunk and branches (Dec–Feb).

Habitat: Rocky outcrops in grassland and also in evergreen, forest near rivers in Zimbabwe.

Ecological notes: The fruits are eaten by birds, animals and people, and are used to make jelly, syrup and wine. The roots are eaten by bushpigs. Fruits and roots are used in traditional medicine.

Gardening: Slow growing, from seed or cuttings. Drought resistant and fairly cold resistant.

Similar species: Natal Milkplum (582) *Englerophytum natalense* (= *Bequaertiodendron natalense*), (4–20 m) has horizontal branches; it is found in coastal forests. The leaves are silvery beneath, fruits are not densely crowded.

Erythrina lysistemon

African names:
Gewone Koraalboom (A); mmalê (NS); umsinsi (Sw, X, Z).

Height: A small to medium-sized (3–12 m), deciduous^G tree with a sturdy trunk. It branches low down and has a sparse, rounded crown. The bare tree is spectacular in winter, when it is covered in scarlet flowers.

Identification: The bark is pale grey-brown and grooved, with scattered, hooked thorns. Leaves are compound with 3 leaflets and with small hooked prickles.

Flowers are bright red and appear in erect, narrow inflorescences^G before the leaves. The stamens^G are enclosed by the long narrow standard petal^G (Jun–Oct). Long, thin, black pods enclose the seeds in compartments, which narrow between the red seeds (Sep–Feb).

Habitat: Woodland and coastal bush areas.

Ecological notes: Leaves and bark are browsed by game and the roots are eaten by bushpigs. Butterflies breed on the tree. The flowers attract insects and birds, and are eaten by monkeys. Used in traditional medicine.

Gardening: Grown from seed, cuttings or truncheons. It is drought resistant and survives light frost.

Similar species: Coast Coral Tree (242) *Erythrina caffra* (10–18 m) has leaves with no prickles. The orange-red flowers are broader; the broad standard petal^G is curved back to display the stamens^G.

Blue Guarri 594

Euclea crispa

African names:
Bloughwarrie (A);
mohlakola (NS);
indvodzemnyama
(Sw); umgwali (X);
umshekisane (X, Z);
idungamuzi,
umnqundane (Z).

Height: An evergreen^G shrub or small to medium-sized tree (2–5 m, can reach 10 m), with low spreading branches and a dense grey-green crown. The shape is quite variable.

Identification: The bark is rough and dark grey. Young growth is rusty red. Leaves are opposite and leathery and bluish-green above, 15–50 x 5–15 mm. Flowers are small and scented, occurring in branched inflorescences^G, up to 30 mm long. Male and female flowers occur on separate trees (Dec–May). Fruits are brownish-black and small, 5 mm in diameter, round and hard (May–Dec).

Habitat: Woodland, rocky hillsides in grassland and on forest margins.

Ecological notes: The bark and leaves are browsed by black rhino. Fruits are eaten by birds, rats, mongooses, antelope and people. Branches are used to beat out fires and twigs are used as toothbrushes. Roots are used to make dark brown dye for basket weaving. The bark, leaves and fruit are used in traditional medicine.

Gardening: Grown from seed, it is drought and frost resistant.

Similar species: Common Guarri (601) *Euclea undulata*, is a small tree or multi-stemmed shrub with small leaves (20–30 mm), which are broader in the upper half. The flowers are in short unbranched inflorescences^G.

Common Tree Euphorbia

Euphorbia ingens

African names:
Gewone Naboom
(A); mokgoro (NS);
umhlonhlo (Sw, Z).

Height: A medium-sized (7–10 m),
succulent tree with a short, stout
trunk and a single massive crown.

Identification: Lower branches
persist and are not shed with age.
The square branches, usually
4-angled, narrow at irregular
intervals to form distinct joints.
A copious milky latex is evident
when the branches are broken.
Fruits are round and reddish-mauve
in colour, up to 15 mm in diameter,
and are borne on long stalks, up
to 45 mm long (Aug–Oct).

Habitat: Woodland.

Ecological notes: Monkeys eat the
fruits and the seeds are eaten by
birds. Roots are eaten by cane rats
and porcupines. The milky sap
although very poisonous to people
is used in traditional medicine and
as a fish poison. The timber is soft
and of no value.

Gardening: A useful feature and
container plant, it is grown from
seed or cuttings.

Similar species: Transvaal
Candelabra Tree (346) *Euphorbia
cooperi* (up to 7 m) has a
candelabra-shaped crown; the
side branches, which have large
triangular 5–6 angled segments,
die off each year, leaving the
main stem bare for up to 3 m.
The fruit is a 3-lobed capsule.

Transvaal Beech

Faurea saligna

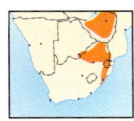

African names:
Transvaalboeken-
hout (A); mongêna
(NS); isicalaba (Sw);
umcalathole (Z).

Height: A small to medium-sized
(6–8 m, can reach 18 m), semi-
deciduous tree with a straight trunk,
narrow crown and drooping leaves.

Identification: The bark is dark
grey-black and deeply grooved.
Leaves are long and narrow, up to
150 x 20 mm, with wavy margins
and reddish leaf stalks. Young
branchlets, new leaves and autumn
leaves are reddish. The creamy
green, stalkless flowers are in long,
hanging, honey-scented spikes[G],
up to 150 x 30 mm (Oct–Jan).
Fruiting spikes[G] are pinkish-white,
and the nutlet[G] is covered with
silvery hairs (Nov–Apr).

Habitat: Woodland, on well-
drained soils, often in colonies.

Ecological notes: The durable,
beautifully grained timber is used

in cabinet making, the wood is
termite resistant and is also used
for firewood. The bark is used for
tanning leather.

Gardening: Slow growing,
usually from seed.

Similar species: Forest Beech (73),
Faurea galpinii, is found in high
altitude mistbelt forest. The leaves
are broader and the flower spikes[G]
held erect.

Large-leaved Rock Fig 63

Ficus abutilifolia (=F. soldanella)

African names: Grootblaarrotsvy (A); mphaya (NS); impayi, inkokhokho, ubambematsheni (Z).

Height: A small, deciduous 'rock-splitting' tree (2–10 m) with a conspicuous yellowish-white trunk and roots, and a sparse crown.

Identification: The bark is smooth, and the ends of the twigs are thick, 10 mm in diameter. Leaves are thick, large and heart-shaped, up to 160 x 250 mm, shiny dark green with yellow veins, and hairless; the leaf stalks are 25–180 mm long. The round, red figs, 10–25 mm in diameter, are clustered towards the tips of the twigs (Sep–Mar).

Habitat: Cliffs and rocky hills in woodland.

Ecological notes: The tasty fruits are eaten by birds, monkeys, baboons and antelope. The leaves are used in traditional medicine.

Gardening: Grown from seed and cuttings, it is frost sensitive.

Similar species: Small-leaved Rock Fig (62) *Ficus tettensis* (5–7 m) has smooth white bark and hairy branchlets. The small, hairy leaves are heart- to kidney-shaped, 35–90 x 30–115 mm, and have short stalks up to 30 mm long. The hairy, red figs are small, 7–10 mm in diameter.

Common Wild Fig 48

Ficus thonningii

African names: Gewone Wurgvy (A); moumo (NS); umthombe (X, Z); umbombe (Z).

Height: A medium to large (10–20 m), evergreen^G tree with a broad trunk and a dense, spreading crown. It starts life as a 'strangler' on other trees or rocks and has fine aerial roots.

Identification: The bark is smooth and grey. Leaves vary in size and shape, 50–100 x 10–40 mm, and are shiny and dark green in colour with a rounded to tapering tip and a long leaf stalk, 7–45 mm. Figs are small, red and hairy, 10 mm in diameter, and are usually stalkless (throughout the year, usually Aug–Dec).

Habitat: Woodland and along forest margins.

Ecological notes: The leaves and twigs are eaten by game. The fruits attract insects and are eaten by birds and animals; and can be made into a jam. Butterflies breed on this tree. The timber can be used for planks and the bark fibre for weaving and making twine. Used in traditional medicine.

Gardening: Quick growing, from cuttings and truncheons, it is sensitive to cold.

Similar species: Natal Fig (57) *Ficus natalensis*, has leaves with rounded or blunt tips and short leaf stalks, 4–10 mm. The hairless figs have stalks up to 7 mm long. Forest Fig (52) *Ficus craterostoma*, has leaf tips that are blunt to indented.

Common Cluster Fig 66

Ficus sycomorus

African names: Gewone trosvy, Rivierwildevy (A); mogobôya (NS); umkhiwubovane (Sw); umkhiwane (Z).

Height: A magnificent semi-deciduous[G] tree (10–35 m) with a huge buttressed trunk and a widely spreading crown.

Identification: The bark is pale yellowish-orange, powdery or flaking. A milky latex or sap is present. Leaves are large, 50–200 x 30–150 mm, thin and hard with a rough and hairy texture. Figs are yellowish-red and large, 20–50 mm in diameter, and are produced in large bunches off the main branches (year round).

Habitat: Riverine vegetation, often in groves.

Ecological notes: The leaves are highly nutritious for livestock. The figs attract fruit- and insect-eating birds. Bats, monkeys, baboons, bushpigs, antelope and people eat the fruit. The bark and milky sap are used in traditional medicine. The wood is soft, and is used for carving drums; rope is made from the inner bark.

Gardening: Grown from seed and truncheons, it needs plentiful water. It is frost sensitive.

Similar species: Broom Cluster Fig (50) *Ficus sur*, has smooth, white to grey bark and shiny, coppery new leaves in spring. The mature leaves are smooth, hairless and grey-green, with irregularly toothed margins.

Tree Pincushion

Leucospermum conocarpodendron

African names:
Kreupelhout (A).

Height: A shrub or small tree (3–6 m) with a rounded, compact crown.

Identification: The branches are gnarled and interlocking. Leaves are oblong, tapering to the base; the tips are rounded with 3–10 reddish teeth. The leaves are variable: those of the subsp.

conocarpodendron are woolly and greyish-silver in colour, while the leaves of the subsp. *viridum* are deep green and smooth. Flowers form yellow flowerheads^G, up to 88 mm in diameter (Aug–Jan).

Habitat: South West Cape mountains and coastal dunes, in fynbos, often in dense stands.

Ecological notes: The bark was once used in tanning leather. The wood is used for firewood. The flowers are harvested as attractive cut-flowers.

Gardening: Grown from seed. It is drought resistant at the coast.

Similar species: Common Pincushion (84.2) *Leucospermum cuneiforme*, is usually a multi-stemmed shrub; the bark has warty lumps at the base of the stems. The long, narrow leaves have flat tips with 3 teeth. The flowers are yellow to red.

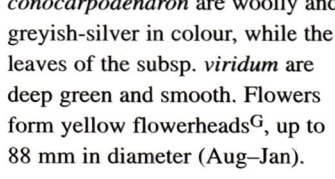

Apple-leaf

Lonchocarpus capassa

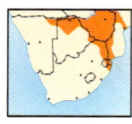

African names: Appelblaar (A); mphata (NS); isi-homohomo (Sw, Z); umbhandu (Z).

Height: A small to medium-sized (5–15 m) tree with a tall, slightly twisted trunk and a sparse crown.

Identification: The bark is light grey-brown and flaking. Leaves are compound and have 1–3 pairs of leaflets, and a large terminal one, up to 150 x 100 mm. Leaflets are hard, shiny green above and velvety grey-green below. Mauve flowers form dense sprays, up to 150 mm long, which are scented (Sep–Dec). Pods are large, flat and light grey-brown (Jul–Aug).

Habitat: Woodland and wooded grassland.

Ecological notes: The leaves are browsed by livestock and game. Pollen and nectar attract bees.

Butterflies breed on this tree. Sap-sucking 'spittle bugs' living on the tree excrete a waste liquid making the tree appear to 'drip rain' at certain times of the year. The timber is used for carving and dugout canoes. Leaves and roots are used in traditional medicine.

Status: Protected.

Gardening: Fast growing from seed, in frost free areas.

Similar species: Narrow Lance-pod (238.1) *Lonchocarpus bussei* (up to 10 m) is found mostly from Zimbabwe northwards. It has 3–7 smaller leaflets, 40–70 mm long.

Coastal Red Milkwood

Mimusops caffra

African names: Kusrooimelkhout (A); umthunzi (X, Z); umhayihayi, umnole amasethole (Z).

Height: An evergreen^G shrub or small to medium-sized tree (4–10 m, can reach 25 m), with a dense spreading crown. The trunk is tall and broad in forest but short, twisted or bent and branching low down in exposed places. It grows as a stunted, low-growing shrub in areas with heavy salt spray.

Identification: The bark is rough, dark grey and grooved. A milky latex or sap is present. Leaves are alternate, small, 30–70 x 15–40 mm, hard and leathery with blue-green above and whitish hairs beneath. The margins are rolled under and the tips are rounded or square, and often notched. Flowers are small, creamy white in colour and occur in small clusters (Jun–Oct). Fruits are oval and red and have rounded tips (Jun–Jan).

Habitat: Dune forest and vegetation, from the high tide mark inland.

Ecological notes: The fruits attract birds, animals and people. The timber is hard, and sticks are used to build huts, boats and fish traps. Butterflies breed on the tree.

Gardening: Grown from seed, it is salt spray resistant.

Similar species: Red Milkwood (584) *Mimusops obovata* (4–20 m) has oval, thin, leathery leaves and orange-red fruits, 35 x 20 mm.

Wild Olive

Olea europaea subsp. *africana*

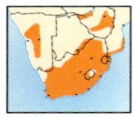

African names:
Olienhout (A);
mohlwane (NS);
umnqumo (X, Z).

Height: An evergreen^G, small to medium-sized (5–14 m) tree. In the open, the trunk is gnarled and twisted. In forest it is tall with a widely spreading crown.

Identification: The bark is rough and dark grey. Leaves are opposite and variable, 20–100 x 17–71 mm, dark green above, silvery-grey below with indistinct veins. The small, scented flowers are in loose inflorescences^G, up to 60 mm long (Oct–Feb). Fruits are oval, up to 10 x 8 mm, and ripen black (Mar–Aug).

Habitat: Widespread, mostly found in woodland.

Ecological notes: Fresh and fallen leaves are eaten by livestock and game. Fruits are eaten by birds, animals and people. Leaves and bark are used in traditional medicine. The termite resistant timber is popular for furniture and carving; the fruit sap is used as ink.

Status: Protected in Northern Cape, Free State and Northwest Province.

Gardening: Grown from seed for gardens, street trees and bonsai. Drought and frost resistant.

Similar species: False Olive (636) *Buddleja saligna* (2–7 m) has longitudinally grooved bark. The grey-green, drooping leaves are white and prominently veined below. The flowers are in dense, branched inflorescences^G, up to 120 mm in diameter (Aug–Jan).

Weeping Wattle

Peltophorum africanum

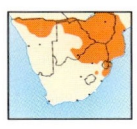

African names:
Huilboom (A);
mosehla (NS);
isikhabakhombe
(Sw, Z); umthobo,
umsehle (Z).

Height: A small to medium-sized
(4–8 m, can reach 15 m)
deciduous^G tree often multi-
stemmed, branching low down,
with a dense, spreading crown.

Identification: The bark is rough
and grey-brown. Reddish-brown
hairs cover the young branchlets,
leaf and flower stalks, sepals^G
and pods. Leaves are compound
with small leaflets, 7 x 2 mm,
and a feathery appearance.
Flowers have crinkled petals^G
and are held in beautiful erect,
yellow sprays or inflorescences^G,
up to 150 x 80 mm (Sep–Apr).
Pods are flat, velvety at first,
becoming smooth and woody
(Dec–May).

Habitat: Woodland and wooded
grassland areas.

Ecological notes: The leaves are
browsed by livestock and game,
the bark is stripped by black rhino
and the pods are eaten by cattle.
Butterflies breed on the tree, and
the flowers attract insects, which
in turn attract birds. Sap-sucking
spittle bugs excrete waste liquid
which weeps from the tree. The
bark and roots are used in
traditional medicine and the timber
is used for carving and firewood.

Gardening: Fast growing, from
seed. Fairly drought resistant.

Wild Date Palm

Phoenix reclinata

African names:
Wildedadelpalm (A);
mopalamo (NS);
lisundvu (Sw);
idama, isundu (X, Z).

Height: A slender (3–12 m), erect or reclining, multi-stemmed palm.

Identification: Leaves are long, feather-shaped and arching (2–4 m long); they are shiny green and have long spines at the base of the leaf stalk. Male and female flowers are on separate trees; the male flowers in large, creamy white bunches (Aug–Nov). Fruits are small, up to 15 mm long, oval and luminous orange, forming large bunches, which ripen brown (Feb–May).

Habitat: Near water and in coastal grassland areas.

Ecological notes: The leaves are browsed by elephants. The small fruits taste like cultivated dates and attract insects, birds, animals and people. The sap is tapped to make

beer, fruiting stems are used for brooms, and leaves for weaving. Used in traditional medicine.

Status: Protected.

Gardening: Grown from seed or suckers, it is drought resistant.

Similar species: Lala Palm (23) *Hyphaene coriacea* (3–7 m) grows in clumps. The greyish leaves are fan-shaped and the large, shiny, dark brown fruits are pear-shaped, 40–60 mm in diameter. Real Fan Palm (24) *Hyphaene petersiana* (up to 20 m) has a single stem; the fruits are round.

Podocarpus falcatus (=Afrocarpus falcatus)

African names: Outeniekwageelhout (A); mogôbagôba (NS); umsonti (Sw, Z); umkhoba (X); umgeya (X, Z).

Height: A medium to very tall tree (10–45 m, can reach 60 m). Evergreen^G with a broad, straight trunk and a fine spreading crown.

Identification: The purplish bark flakes off in round or rectangular patches on mature trees. Leaves are small, bluish- to yellowish-green and leathery; they are narrow and slightly sickle-shaped, 30–50 x 3–5 mm. Mature leaves have a twist at the base. Male trees produce small, scaly cones, about 10 x 3 mm, while female trees produce fleshy, round, yellow fruits, 15 mm in diameter (Dec–Jun).

Habitat: Evergreen^G forest.

Ecological notes: Fruits are eaten by birds, monkeys and bushpigs. The pale yellow timber is fine-grained and hard and is used for furniture and building. Used in traditional medicine. It is the tallest tree in South Africa.

Status: Protected.

Gardening: Quick growing, from seed. It is frost resistant.

Similar species: Real Yellowwood (18) *Podocarpus latifolius* (10–30 m) has longitudinally grooved bark, peeling in strips; the leaves are held horizontally, 60–150 x 5–13 mm. The fleshy, purplish-red fruits have 1 or 2 purplish seeds, up to 15 mm in diameter.

Common Sugarbush

Protea caffra

African names:
Gewone Suikerbos
(A); mogalagala
(NS); isiqwane,
indlunge (Sw, X);
isiqalaba (X, Z);
uhlinkihlane (Z).

Height: A shrub or small (3–8 m)
tree with a single trunk (or multi-
stemmed) and rounded crown.

Identification: The bark is thick,
black and grooved. Young stems
are smooth, pinkish-green and the
long, narrow leaves (up to 250 x
45 mm) are leathery and hairless;
pale yellowish to blue-green. The
cream to pink or reddish flowerheads[G], 45–80 mm in diameter,
are scented (Oct–Mar).

Habitat: The most widespread
Protea sp. in South Africa, found
in wooded grassland and on rocky
ridges, often in large colonies.

Ecological notes: The nectar
attracts birds and insects. Butterflies
breed on the tree. The wood makes
excellent firewood, and the bark is
used in traditional medicine.

Gardening: Grown from seed, it
is fire and frost
resistant.

Similar species:
Wagon Tree (86)
Protea nitida, is a
gnarled shrub or
small tree (up to
5 m), in fynbos.
The solitary
flowerheads[G] are
creamy white, up
to 160 x 20 mm.

Kiaat/Wild Teak

Pterocarpus angolensis

African names: Kiaat (A); morôtô (NS); umvangazi (Sw, Z); mukwa (Zimbabwe).

Height: A medium to large (5–13 m, can reach up to 30 m) deciduous[G] tree with a tall trunk and a sparse, spreading crown of drooping leaves.

Identification: The bark is dark grey-brown and rough. Leaves are compound and have 5–9 pairs of leaflets, 25–70 x 20–45 mm, and a terminal one. The fragrant, yellow flowers hang in branched sprays (Aug–Feb). Pods are distinctive: large, up to 150 mm in diameter, round and pale brown with a broad flat wing and long stiff bristles in the central part of the pod (Jan–Jun).

Habitat: Woodland.

Ecological notes: The leaves are browsed by game and the flowers attract bees. Butterflies breed on the tree. Pods are eaten by baboons, monkeys and squirrels. The timber is used for building, furniture and carving and the red sap is used as a dye. Bark and root are used in traditional medicine.

Status: Protected.

Gardening: Grown from seed or truncheons, it is sensitive to frost.

Similar species: Round-leaved Teak (237) *Pterocarpus rotundifolius* (3–9 m) has 1–3 pairs of large leaflets, up to 150 x 110 mm, and a terminal one. The yellow flowers cover the tree in large erect sprays. The pods have no bristles.

Quinine Tree

Rauvolfia caffra

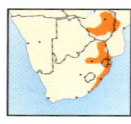

African names: Kinaboom (A); monadi (NS); umfomamasi (Sw); umjelo (X); umhlambamanzi (Z).

Height: A medium to large (7–15 m, can reach 20 m) deciduous[G] tree with a tall, straight trunk and a large spreading canopy.

Identification: The bark is thinly corky and yellowish-brown. A milky latex or sap is present. Leaves are large and glossy green with translucent veins, 120–280 x 30–60 mm. Flowers are small, white and borne in branched inflorescences[G], up to 200 mm in diameter (May–Oct). The fleshy, green fruits, 15 mm in diameter, become wrinkled and black with age (Oct–Mar).

Habitat: Riverine forest and woodland areas.

Ecological notes: Leaves are browsed by game. Flowers and fruits attract monkeys, bushbabies, birds and insects. The timber is used for drums and kitchen utensils. The sap, bark and roots are used in traditional medicine.

Status: Protected.

Gardening: Grown from seed or cuttings. Sensitive to frost.

Similar species: Matumi (684), *Breonadia salicina* (up to 40 m) has rough, grooved bark and no milky latex or sap. The leaf veins are yellow. The flowers are in small compact flowerheads[G], up to 40 mm in diameter.

Karree

Rhus lancea

African names: Karee (A); mokalabata (NS).

Height: A small to medium-sized (2–9 m), evergreen^G tree; single-stemmed (or multi-stemmed), with a loose, drooping, rounded crown.

Identification: The bark is rough, grooved and dark brown. Leaves are compound with 3 long, slender, leathery leaflets, up to 150 x 12 mm; dark olive-green above and paler beneath. The small, greenish-yellow flowers are in clusters, up to 60 mm long; male and female flowers on separate trees (Jun–Sep). Fruits are small, roundish and glossy brown (Sep–Jan).

Habitat: Widespread in woodland (except in KwaZulu-Natal).

Ecological notes: The leaves are browsed by livestock and game and the fruits are eaten by birds. The hard, durable timber is used for fence posts.

Status: Protected in Northern Cape and parts of the Free State.

Gardening: A hardy, popular garden and street tree, it is easily grown from seed or cuttings. Drought and frost resistant.

Similar species: White Karree (396) *Rhus pendulina* (=*R. viminales*), (up to 10 m) the bark is pale and flaky when old, and the stems often spiny. The bright green leaves are thin and the fruits round and reddish, drying black. In the wild it is restricted to arid areas of the Orange River Catchment.

Weeping Boer-bean

Schotia brachypetala

African names:
Huilboerboon (A);
molope (NS);
uvovovo (Sw, Z);
umgxamu (X, Z);
ihluze (Z).

Height: A medium to large (3–25 m), semi-deciduous^G tree with a broad trunk, and a dense, spreading, rounded crown. It has spectacular deep red flowers, especially evident before the new leaves appear.

Identification: The bark is rough and grey-brown. Leaves are compound, with 4–6 pairs of shiny, dark green leaflets, 25–80 x 40 mm, which are unequal-sided at the base.

The dense clusters of flowers appear mainly on old wood; their petals^G are reduced and thread-like (Aug–Nov). Pods are flat, woody and dark brown; the large, brown seeds have a light yellow aril^G (Jan–May).

Habitat: Woodland and on streambanks and termitaria.

Ecological notes: The leaves are browsed by game. The flowers produce copious nectar and attract insects, birds and monkeys. The timber is used for furniture, flooring and firewood, and the bark as a dye. Sap-sucking spittle bugs excrete waste liquid which weeps from the tree. Bark and roots are used in traditional medicine.

Gardening: It is grown from seed, flowering when quite young. It withstands drought and mild frost.

Similar species: Bush Boer-bean (204) *Schotia latifolia*, has similar leaves; the petals^G are well developed and pale pink in colour.

Marula 360

Sclerocarya birrea subsp. *caffra*

African names: Maroela (A); morula (NS); umganu (Sw, Z).

Height: A medium to large (7–18 m), deciduous[G] tree with a broad, straight trunk and a widely spreading, rounded crown.

Identification: The bark is flaky and the twigs are thick-tipped. Leaves are compound with 3–7 pairs of leaflets and a terminal one, 30–100 x 15–40 mm. On young plants the leaflets have toothed margins. Flowers are small, pinkish-red, and male and female flowers occur on separate trees (Sep–Nov). Fruits are large and fleshy, up to 40 mm in diameter, and ripen yellow (Jan–Mar).

Habitat: Woodland.

Ecological notes: The leaves are browsed by game, and the bark is stripped by elephants. The flowers attract insects. The fruits are eaten by livestock, game, monkeys,

baboons and people; are used to brew an alcoholic drink and to make a delicious jelly preserve; the tasty nut-like kernels are eaten. The bark is used in traditional medicine. Butterflies and moths breed on the tree. The timber is used for carvings and firewood, and the bark is used to make a dye.

Gardening: It is quick growing from seed or truncheons.

Tamboti 341

Spirostachys africana

African names: Tambotie (A); morekuri (NS); umthombothi (Sw, Z).

Height: A medium-sized (5–10 m, can reach 16 m) deciduous[G] tree with a tall, straight trunk and rounded crown.

Identification: The bark is blackish and cracked into rectangular blocks. The young branches are spiny. A milky latex or sap is present. Leaves are small, 35–70 x 18–35 mm, dull green and have scalloped margins. Autumn leaves turn yellow to red. Flowers are very small and are clustered in short spikes[G] (Jul–Jan). Fruits are 3-lobed woody capsules, 10 mm in diameter, and are often infested with the pupae of a moth causing them to jump once they have fallen from the tree (Oct–Feb), hence their name 'jumping beans'.

Habitat: Woodland, often in pure stands on heavy soils.

Ecological notes: Leaves are browsed by livestock, game and monkeys; porcupines eat the bark. Dropped fruits are eaten by birds. The beautifully grained, pleasantly scented wood makes a very hard timber and is used for furniture and building. The milky latex or sap is very toxic causing extreme nausea especially when heated. The sawdust can blind a person. The bark and latex or sap are used in traditional medicine.

Status: Protected in South Africa.

Gardening: Grown from fresh seed, not frost resistant.

Black Monkey Orange 626

Strychnos madagascariensis

African names: Swartklapper (A); mookgwane (NS); umkwakwa (Sw, Z).

Height: A small, multi-stemmed (3–8 m), deciduous[G] tree with a short trunk and a densely branched, spreading canopy.

Identification: The bark is smooth and pale grey to brown. Leaves are thick, leathery and opposite, shiny dark green above and paler beneath with 3–5 veins from the base. Leaves are either velvety on both surfaces or only on the veins below. Fruits are large, round and woody, about 80 mm in diameter, and are grey-green ripening orange. The large seeds are covered in orange pulp (Mar–Aug).

Habitat: Woodland and coastal bush.

Ecological notes: The leaves and fruits are eaten by livestock and game, the seeds by birds and squirrels. Rural people remove the slimy pulp from the seeds, dry it and store it for later use. The pulp is sometimes made into a drink. The wood is used for firewood.

Gardening: Grown from seed, it is drought resistant.

Similar species: Green Monkey Orange (629) *Strychnos spinosa* (3–7 m) has stems with slender, paired spines. The fruit is bigger, up to 120 mm in diameter, and is green, turning yellow-brown when ripe. The tasty, slimy, brown pulp is eaten fresh.

Waterberry

Syzygium cordatum

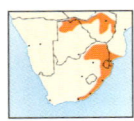

African names:
Waterbessie (A);
montlho (NS);
umncozi (Sw);
umjomi, umswi (X);
umdoni (Z).

Height: A medium to large (5–12 m, can reach 20 m), evergreen[G] tree with a sturdy, crooked trunk and a dense, spreading, rounded crown.

Identification: The bark is smooth becoming rough and pale to dark grey with age. Twigs are 4-angled. Leaves are bluish-green, oval to roundish, 25–100 x 19–80 mm, and opposite; they are thick and leathery, and the base is often deeply lobed and clasping the stalk. Leaf stalks are short or absent. Crushed leaves smell of eucalyptus oil. The conspicuous fluffy white flowers are in bunches (up to 100 mm in diameter) (Aug–Nov). Fruits are fleshy, oval, and purplish-black, up to 20 x 10 mm (Nov–Mar).

Habitat: Woodland, forest, often near water.

Ecological notes: The leaves are browsed by game and the flowers attract insects. Butterflies breed on the tree. The fruits are eaten by birds, animals and people. The bark is used to make a red-brown dye and the durable timber is used for boat building and firewood. Used in traditional medicine.

Status: Protected.

Gardening: It is fast growing, from seed. Cold resistant but is sensitive to frost.

Similar species: Forest Water Berry (556) *Syzygium gerrardii* (15–30 m) is a forest tree with a buttressed trunk. The leaves have a distinct stalk and taper to a long, narrow tip. The fruits are roundish.

Silver Clusterleaf 551

Terminalia sericea

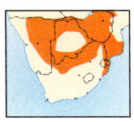

African names:
Vaalboom (A);
mogônônô (NS);
umkhonono (Sw, Z).

Height: A small to medium-sized (4–10 m), deciduous[G] tree with horizontal branching and a spreading, silvery-grey crown.

Identification: The bark is dark grey-brown and deeply grooved. Leaves are greyish and clustered towards the ends of the branchlets, and are long and narrow, 55–120 x 15–45 mm, covered in fine silvery hairs. Flowers are small, greenish-white and clustered in spikes[G]; they are unpleasantly scented (Nov–Jan). Fruits are flat and single-winged, up to 35 x 25 mm, turning pink to dark purplish-red (Mar–May).

Habitat: Woodland, on sandy soils, often in large colonies.

Ecological notes: The leaves are browsed by livestock and game and the flowers attract insects.

Butterflies breed on the tree. The root is used in traditional medicine. The timber is heavy, hard and termite resistant; it is used for building and for firewood.

Gardening: Quick growing, usually from seed. Resistant to light frost and drought.

Similar species: The Lowveld Clusterleaf (550) *Terminalia prunioides*, is multi-stemmed with small, dark green leaves, the tips rounded or notched. The leaves are clustered on short, spike-like side twigs. The fruits are larger, 40–60 mm, and reddish-purple.

Natal Mahogany

Trichilia emetica

African names:
Rooiessenhout (A);
mmaba (NS);
umkhuhlu (Sw, Z).

Height: A medium to tall (10–35 m), evergreen[G] tree with a sturdy trunk and a rounded crown.

Identification: The bark is smooth and grey-brown. The compound leaves are large with 3–5 pairs of leaflets and a terminal one, up to 150 x 50 mm. The creamy green flowers are in dense bunches, and male and female flowers occur on separate trees (Aug–Nov). Fruit is a roundish, pale green capsule, up to 25 mm in diameter, with a distinct neck, up to 30 mm. The large black seeds are almost covered by a red aril[G] (Dec–Apr).

Habitat: Widespread in woodland, coastal areas and riverine forest.

Ecological notes: The leaves are browsed by game. Nectar attracts birds and insects and the fruits attract birds, baboons, monkeys

and antelope. People use the seeds to make a soup. Butterflies breed on the tree. An all-purpose timber, it is also used for drums and dugout canoes. The bark and seeds are used in traditional medicine.

Status: Protected.

Gardening: It is quick growing from seed or cuttings. Drought resistant and frost tender.

Similar species: The Forest Mahogany (300) *Trichilia dregeana*, is confined to high rainfall, coastal and montane forest. The fruits have no neck.

Buffalo Thorn 447

Ziziphus mucronata

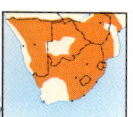

African names: Blinkblaar-wag-'n-bietjie (A); mokgalô (NS); umphafa (Sw, X, Z).

Height: Small to medium-sized (3–10 m, can reach 20 m) semi-deciduous with a broad, crooked trunk and a sparse, spreading crown with drooping branches.

Identification: The bark is grey, rough and cracked into small, peeling strips. The strong, sharp thorns occur in pairs, one straight and one hooked. Older trees have fewer thorns (sometimes none). Leaves are alternate, 30–90 x 20–50 mm, glossy light green with 3 veins from the base; the margins are toothed in the upper two thirds, the base is unequal (asymmetric). Flowers are small and yellowish-green (Oct–Apr). Fruits are reddish-brown berries, up to 15 mm in diameter, with a shiny, leathery skin and a dry, powdery pulp (Feb–Aug).

Habitat: Widespread, mostly in woodland and wooded grassland.

Ecological notes: The leaves are browsed by livestock and game and used with the bark and roots in traditional medicine. The flowers attract insects, which in turn attract birds. Butterflies breed on the tree. Fruits are eaten by birds, mammals and people. The seeds can be used as a coffee substitute. The wood is used as a hard, heavy, all-purpose timber.

Status: Protected in the Free State.

Gardening: It is fast growing from seed. Frost and drought resistant.

Glossary

Aril: Fleshy, sometimes brightly coloured outer covering of a seed.

Bracts: Leaf-like structures at the base of a flower or inflorescence.

Deciduous: Refers to trees that shed leaves at the end of the growing season, usually winter.

Endemic: Describes species that occur naturally in an area and are found nowhere else.

Evergreen: Refers to trees that lose and replace leaves all year long but never all at once.

Flowerhead: A collection of flowers arranged in a tight cluster.

Flower spikes: Long, branch-like structures of tightly clustered or stalkless flowers.

Indigenous: Describes species that occur naturally in an area.

Inflorescence: A structure bearing several individual flowers.

Invasive: Describes an introduced species that is spreading without control.

Lobed: Where a plant organ, usually a leaf, is divided into branching portions or sections.

Midrib: The central portion or main vein of a leaf.

Naturalised: Describes an introduced species that is established but not invasive.

Nutlet: Small nut-like fruit.

Petals: Protective leaf-like flower parts – usually brightly coloured.

Sepals: Protective leaf-like flower parts – usually green in colour.

Stamens: Male reproductive organs that produce pollen.

Standard petal: A large petal usually found on the asymmetrical flowers of plants in the bean family.

Umbel: An upturned, umbrella-shaped, branching structure made up of many individual flowers.

Recommended further reading:

Coates Palgrave, K. (1977). *Trees of Southern Africa*. Struik.

Pooley, E. (1993). *The Complete Field Guide to Trees of Natal, Zululand & Transkei*. Natal Flora Publications Trust.

Pooley, E. (1998). *Trees: Southern African Green Guide*. Southern Book Publishers.

Van Wyk, B. & Van Wyk, P. (1997). *Field Guide to Trees of Southern Africa*. Struik.

Van Wyk, P. (1984). *Field Guide to Trees of the Kruger National Park*. Struik.